Encounter

Copyright © 2016 by Nicole Pritchett

Cover by: Bonnie Mace

ISBN-13: 9781946447036

Lift Bridge Publishing
Printed in U.S.A

Encounter

Learning How to Have a Relationship with God

Study Guide

Author: Nicole Pritchett

Editor: Erica Young- Joyful Editing Services, LLC

Cover Design: Bonnie Mace

Bible Version- NIV

Table of Contents

Introduction

Whether you are reading the Bible or conversing with a friend over coffee, the probability that relationships will be discussed is extremely high. The relationship topic itself is universal, and I would argue, is the reason why it is used countless times in scripture. A relationship is something we can all comprehend, on one level or another, and it can be used to apply meaning and understanding to the context of a variety of issues. To push the thought even further, one could have a negative relationship or a positive relationship with someone and that encounter between the two individuals would have a lasting influence. Considering all the relationships discussed in history and in the context of scriptures, there is one relationship encounter that we can have that will not let us down. In fact, the encounter we have with God will be, or should be, the foundation in which all other relationships are cultivated. Whether you have experienced an encounter with God, are still longing for the encounter, or you are unsure if all of this talk is for real, I challenge you to be vulnerable and honest with yourself in the next several weeks as we discover for some, and rediscover for others, the steps to take that lead to an encounter with God.

There are different types of relationships that construct our perception of what a healthy relationship looks like. One of the first relationships that we get the opportunity to experience in this world is our relationship with our mothers and fathers. The world illustrates, in a variety of ways, that the relationship between a mother and a child is nurturing and filled with opportunities for development. Even when considering how animals mother their newborns, we can confirm the perspective that mothers are created to nurture their offspring. The protection and security of a father is also an identified perception of the nature of a relationship between a father and child. After our parents identify the role in which they will take in our lives, then comes siblings, teachers, coaches, friends, additional family, and employers. These relationships leave imprints on our hearts regarding whether we can trust relationships or whether we live our lives guarded against the pain inflicted on us from these individuals. I believe that whichever is true for us influences, to some degree, how we function in a relationship with God.

In the upcoming weeks of this study, we will explore reading about God, applying what we read, praying, hearing back from God, worshipping Him, walking with Him, and trusting Him. It is important to know that none of these areas can or should be forced, but that you remain honest with yourself and where you are. The growth will come naturally as you allow God to show up in your life. It is great that the eagerness is present and that you want to learn to do all of this right away, but authentic consistency in these areas comes as a result of a relationship. This study is in no way a written in stone method to encounter God. It is simply teachings and revelations that I have received that have helped me Encounter God in ways that are beyond anything I can write to you. This study is written in a way to create a space in which you can critically think and explore with others how to grow in God. There are no answers written in the back of the study because I believe that your answers will be spoken directly to you during your encounter with God.

Week One
God's Perspective

In the introduction, the mention of a variety of different relationships was discussed. As an icebreaker for this first session, discuss some of your views and perceptions of healthy and unhealthy relationships? What is your idea of what God has to say about being in a relationship with you? This first session will be used to set a foundation of what God has to say about you. The reading for today will describe God's perspective on communication, love, freedom, and the promises that come as a result of a relationship with Him.

John 10 New International Version (NIV)

The Good Shepherd and His Sheep

1 "Very truly I tell you Pharisees, anyone who does not enter the sheep pen by the gate, but climbs in by some other way, is a thief and a robber. 2 The one who enters by the gate is the shepherd of the sheep. 3 The gatekeeper opens the gate for him, *and the sheep listen to his voice. He calls his own sheep by name and leads them out. 4 When he has brought out all his own, he goes on ahead of them, and his sheep follow him because they know his voice.* 5 But they will never follow a stranger; in fact, they will run away from him because they do not recognize a stranger's voice." 6 Jesus used this figure of speech, but the Pharisees did not understand what he was telling them.

7 Therefore Jesus said again, "Very truly I tell you, I am the gate for the sheep. 8 All who have come before me are thieves and robbers, but the sheep have not listened to them. 9 I am

the gate; whoever enters through me will be saved. *They will come in and go out, and find pasture.* 10 The thief comes only to steal and kill and destroy; *I have come that they may have life, and have it to the full.*

11 *"I am the good shepherd. The good shepherd lays down his life for the sheep.* 12 The hired hand is not the shepherd and does not own the sheep. So when he sees the wolf coming, he abandons the sheep and runs away. Then the wolf attacks the flock and scatters it. 13 The man runs away because he is a hired hand and cares nothing for the sheep.

14 *"I am the good shepherd; I know my sheep and my sheep know me— 15 just as the Father knows me and I know the Father—and I lay down my life for the sheep.* 16 I have other sheep that are not of this sheep pen. I must bring them also. They too will listen to my voice, and there shall be one flock and one shepherd. 17 The reason my Father loves me is that I lay down my life—only to take it up again. 18 No one takes it from me, but I lay it down of my own accord. I have authority to lay it down and authority to take it up again. This command I received from my Father."

Discussion Questions:

1. What do the words in bold mean to you?

2. How does it make you feel to know they were directed toward you?

3. Have you experienced a relationship with someone in which this context is true?

4. Have you ever had this encounter with God? Describe the experience.

Moment of Honesty:

Of the topics moving forward (*Reading the Bible, Applying the Bible, Praying, Hearing from God, Worshipping God, Walking with God, Trusting God, Encountering God*) reflect on where you are in each area and identify ways in which you can improve. Create an illustration as to what your expectation of an encounter with God will look like when you have reached this place.

Prayer

God, we want to know You more. The relationship encounters that we have had up to now are nothing in comparison to the love and commitment You have for us. As we commit to reading Your Word, teach us how to apply it to our lives. Convict us when we are too lazy to speak to You in the posture of prayer. Help us create the space where we can hear directly from You. Make our ears sensitive to Your voice that will lead us to green pastures. We are but sheep, God, waiting to be led by the Good Shepherd. Distort the voice of the enemy in our lives. We trust that You will do great things in reshaping our path. As we walk with You over the next several weeks, God, show us in individualized ways how You alone are enough. Thank You in advance for the encounter that we are about to experience. As Paul says in Ephesians 3:20, "now unto him who is able to do exceedingly abundantly above what we can ask or think, according to the power that works in us." Amen.

Journal:

_____

_____

_____

_____

_____

_____

_____

_____

_____

_____

Week Two
Reading the Bible

One of the first lessons taught in grade school is reading. The foundations of reading begin as simply learning to identify the letters of the alphabet. Each letter of the alphabet has a purpose, and collectively, they form words that help us understand messages that are being relayed. It's the same with the Bible. When we understand the purpose of the Bible, it becomes less intimidating to read and more adventurous to read. What, then, is the purpose? The purpose of the Bible is to give us an understanding of who God is and what He has set out to accomplish. With that understanding, we can then begin to move forward in embracing the words written in the Bible as an illustration of the heart of a God who wants to be in a relationship with us.

If you are in any generation prior to the millennial generation, you can relate with not getting a blueprint of who someone is before you enter into a relationship with them. If they do give you a verbal blueprint, often times it comes back inconsistent with who they really are. Now to the millennials who are growing up in an era where resumes with characteristics of an individual are posted on every social media and dating site, even then, often times the description of the individual comes back inconsistent. We can trust that what we read about God, in the Bible, will be consistent with who He really is. Isaiah 55:11 reads, "so is my word that goes out from my mouth: It will not return to me empty, but will accomplish what I desire and achieve the purpose for which I sent it."

The next phase of learning to read is the pronunciation of the alphabet sounds in which we learn that some letters have multiple sounds depending on the context in which they are used. The content in the Bible is similar to the next step in reading, whereas the revelation that comes from what you read may change or essentially have new meaning. The world has resources such as English teachers and educational games like *Hooked on Phonics* to teach us how to annunciate words. The kingdom's resources are the Holy Spirit, preachers, teachers, and books of study that are based on the Bible. Additionally, James 1:5 reminds us that if any of us lacks wisdom we should ask God who will generously give it to us without finding fault. In other words, no more excuses. We live in a time where sermons are flooding YouTube and the Bible continues to be the number one, best-selling book. It's up to you to make the effort in utilizing these resources to enhance your reading level!

A child then graduates to putting the letters together to form words, sentences, paragraphs, chapter books, and novels. One of the channels in learning from that point on, within the educational system, is through one's ability to comprehend written material. The new found insight is used to then mold the young mind and help them to begin formulating opinions and perspectives on how to navigate through the following years of their lives. The same holds true for the foundation of an encounter with God. The Bible is a source of collected information that illustrates the heart of God.

It was asked once, in a workshop I attended in college, led by one of my biggest spiritual influencers, Pastor Houston, "How should one approach reading the entire Bible?" The answer was, "The same way you would approach eating an elephant, which is one chunk at a time." He then went on to suggest that any other method would be overwhelming and humanly impossible. Back to our reading fundamental example, the same way an elementary school teacher gradually helps a student learn to read is the same concept with reading the Word of God. Take it a little bit at a time. Eventually, your ability will improve and you will be on your way.

It may help to understand how the Bible is divided before challenging yourself to read it. There are two testaments: The Old Testament and The New Testament. The Old Testament, in a nutshell, is a recording of events that took place before the birth of Christ. It encompasses God's creation, covenant with His people, the fall and mistakes of man, and the list goes on. Many religions are derived from the Old Testament alone. As Christians, it is important to understand that both testaments are critical in explaining the entirety of our faith in Christ Jesus. The New Testament is introduced with the family lineage of Christ and His birth, in which the events recorded thereafter all took place after the birth of Christ. The New Testament encompasses the life, death, and resurrection of Jesus which can be found in the Gospels, which are Matthew, Mark, Luke, and John. Following the Gospels is the Book of Acts which includes an explanation, to say the least, of the establishment of the church and the life of Paul. Following the Book of Acts are epistles or letters to different churches on conduct and how to be unified in Christ. The Bible closes with the Book of Revelation.

The question of where to begin depends on where you are in your faith. As a new believer who wants to understand who Christ is and what He did for you, the Gospels will be where you find that answer. The Book of John may serve you well. There is no right or wrong way to read the Bible; in fact, there are countless *Read the Bible in a Year* studies on bookshelves and app stores. I would challenge you to ponder where you are in your faith and understanding of God. Once that question is answered then you can decide, with the guidance of the Holy Spirit, which book to bite into first.

Group Activity

In groups of 2-3, write down some illustrations of Bible stories you remember, scriptures, books of the Bible, and what you would describe to be the foundation of your faith. The challenge here is to NOT use the Bible. Go only from memory. If you have never read the Bible, what is it that you already know about God and His Son, Jesus Christ?

In Joshua 1:8, God tells Joshua to not let the Book of the Law depart from his mouth, but that he is to meditate on it day and night, so that he may be careful to do everything that is written in it. In order to be prosperous and successful, we have to know the Word of God. Just like the elementary student, our knowledge begins with reading and comprehending.

Discussion Questions:

1. How did this exercise make you feel?

2. Are you surprised by how much you know?

3. What does meditating on the Word of God day and night look like to you?

4. What are some strategies that would challenge you or hold you accountable in reading the Bible?

5. Is there someone in your group that you could partner with this week in order to challenge each other to read God's Word?

Challenge

Read a chapter of the Bible, this week, and in the journal section, write down what you comprehend.

Moment of Honesty:

Are you able to hold yourself accountable in reading the Word of God regularly? Do you have an accountability partner? Do you have someone in your life that you challenge, as well as someone who you can go to for spiritual questions?

Memory Verse:

Joshua 1:8

Prayer:

God, thank You for allowing the Word of God to be accessible to us that we may know You more. Forgive us in our negligence in reading the Bible consistently. We accept the command that You gave to Joshua to meditate on Your Word day and night. Your servant James also challenges us in his first chapter that if any of us lacks wisdom we can ask You for it and You will generously give it to us without finding fault in us. With that in mind, thank You God for meeting us where we are and not judging us for not being where we could be. You are a patient God and the greatest teacher known. We understand, though, that when we ask for this wisdom we cannot doubt, so we stand on every word we read and we believe that Your Word is true. Meet us this week in the place we carve out to read Your Word. Speak to us in very unique ways that we may be overwhelmed by Your presence. Provide us the accountability and the assistance we need to understand. We ask this in Your Son, Jesus' name. Amen.

Journal:

_____

_____

_____

_____

_____

_____

_____

_____

_____

_____

Last Week Flashback

How was the last challenge difficult for you based on where you are with God? As a believer, did you find it hard to JUST read and write down what you understood about the passage? As an encounter seeker, did you not understand what you read or desire to read more? As an unbeliever, did you believe or not believe what you read?

Week Three
Applying the Bible

Application, by definition, is the act of putting to use or a use in which something is put. At some point in your life, you had to apply something that was learned. Matthew 7:24-29 provides an illustration about two different kinds of builders: one whose house weathers the storm and the other whose house is crushed by waves. Regardless of the path the builders chose to take, both of them were, in fact, builders. We, too, are builders. We are building a life with each thought we think, each decision we make, and every step we take throughout the day. The question is, are you being tossed and crushed or are you withstanding the storms of life? Applying the Word of God is the key to building a stable foundation and relationship with God.

Say, for instance, a mother gives her child a key to their house and informs the child that she will not be home to let him in. She gives him instruction to put the key in the doorknob and turn it to the right to get into the house. The mother, therefore, granted the child full access to this place of refuge. It is completely up to the child to apply what his mother has instructed him in order to enter into the safe-keeping of their home.

What does this have to do with us applying the Word? God has given us the privilege to have an answer book on how to navigate through life and increase our knowledge of Him. In comparison to the child, to enter into His place of refuge, we have to apply and put to use, the instructions He has given us through His Word. Does this sound familiar? In the first week, we read John 10:3, "the gatekeeper opens the gate for him, and the sheep listen to his voice. He calls his own sheep by name and leads them out. 4 When he has brought out all his own, he goes on ahead of them, and his sheep follow him because they know his voice."

Going back to the builders in Matthew 7, it reads, "therefore everyone who hears these words of mine and puts them into practice is like a wise man who built his house on the rock." Okay, let's assume you agree with taking the path of building on a rock and not sand. How do you, "put these things into practice?" Matthew 5-7 gives several application options for you to try. Let's take a look at an example:

Matthew 6:25

"Do Not Worry"

Read. "Therefore I tell you, do not worry about your life, what you will eat or drink; or about your body, what you will wear."

Comprehend. One way to comprehend this scripture in its literal sense is to not worry about food, drink, and clothing. Another way it can be comprehended is to not worry about basic essential needs.

Depending on where you are in your faith will determine how you perceive this text. The key, here, is to put it into practice. An example of applying this scripture would be to wake up in the morning, thanking God for giving you food, drink, and clothes, or wake up thanking God for giving you your basic needs. Maybe it's your car and gas that gets you to a job that is 40 minutes away. Next year, read it again, gain new insight, and apply it. Watch God reveal more about scripture, and put it into practice. Another example of God using the same instrument for different purposes is how Moses' staff, in Exodus 3, was used for tending sheep. Then in chapter 14, God revealed a new perspective to Moses and told him to use it to part the Red Sea. Be careful not to compare yourself to others during this challenge. The beauty of the encounter you will experience with God is that He knows you and will speak directly to your unique situation. Allow God into that vulnerable place as you read the scripture with your heart, mind, and eyes wide open.

Discussion Questions:

1. Using the passages you read last week, discuss with the group how they can be applied to an area of your life right now or in the future.

2. Practice reading and applying what you read with the topics from Matthew 5-7. In a large group, create groups of 2-3 people and separate the topics, giving one topic to each group. Come back together and have a representative share with the group how these areas can be applied to our lives today.

Challenge:

Read Psalm 119, using whatever method works for you in meditating on the Word day and night. (Use sticky notes, dry erase markers on your mirror, index cards in your car, screensavers, etc.) Select a few verses that will help you hold yourself accountable for reading and applying the Bible. Then, choose one scripture from anywhere in the Bible, this week, that can be applied to your current circumstances. Inform your accountability partner. Read and apply what you have read.

Moment of Honesty:

Are you being tossed and crushed by the storms of life? Or, are you able to withstand the storms of life by applying the Word to your circumstances? Do you believe that every answer you need is in the Bible?

Memory Verse:

Psalm 119: 106

Prayer:

God, thank You for teaching us how to apply what we comprehend. Help us to increase our comfort when it comes to asking You for wisdom unashamed. You are generous, God, to give us the wisdom we ask for, if we dare to believe. Help us this week to continue meditating on Your Word and to engage in application. It is through our knowledge of You that we will recognize You during the encounter we are chasing after. Expose us to Your truths and help us create a habit of applying every Word to our lives. In that, God, we can move forward in prayer and hearing from You. Thank You for Your presence God, and as the psalmist declared, may our tongues sing of Your word, for all Your commands are righteous. May Your hand be ready to help us for we are choosing Your precepts. We long for Your salvation, O Lord, and Your law is our delight. Let us live that we may praise You and may Your laws sustain us. Amen.

Journal:

_____

_____

_____

_____

_____

_____

_____

_____

_____

_____

Last Week Flashback

Which verses, in Psalm 119, did you favor last week? Are there any new strategies you found to be helpful in meditating on what you read? What challenges do you still have in applying the Word of God? Are there any suggestions regarding how to address those challenges?

Week Four
Praying

When I think of the aspects of faith collectively, my favorite aspect is prayer! A songwriter penned these words, "Oh what peace we often forfeit, oh what needless pain we bear, all because we do not carry everything to God in prayer." In light of that hymn, the scripture also says, in Philippians 4:6, "Do not be anxious about anything, but In every situation, by prayer and petition, with thanksgiving, present your requests to God." Prayer is a privilege and a peacemaker. An understanding that will come from reading the Bible is that sin prevented us from having direct access to God's presence. You will find in the Old Testament that a temple was built very strategically and there were many guidelines and requirements set in place for one to enter into the presence of God. You can find this beginning in Exodus 26.

For the sake of this lesson, we will not go into detail about the temple itself. What is encouraged to be understood, however, is the seriousness of the privilege we have to enjoy an intimate encounter with God through prayer. Fast forward through the Bible to Mark's account in the New Testament; chapter 15:37-38 indicates that when Jesus took His last breath on the cross, the curtain of the temple was torn in two, from the top to the bottom.

The tearing of the temple veil was God giving all of us full access to His presence through the death of Jesus. The challenge, then, is to believe this truth and reverence prayer as the privilege that it is. The same way that crowds rush through the doors of store openings and sales is the same urgency and excitement we should have when approaching God. Hebrews 4:16 supports this in saying, "Let us then approach God's throne of grace with confidence, so that we may receive mercy and find grace to help us in our time of need." Now that we have found the space and hopefully gained confidence that God opened the door for us to enter into His presence, we can move into a discussion of how to pray.

Matthew 6: 9-13 New International Version
9 "This, then, is how you should pray:
"'Our Father in heaven, hallowed be your
name, *(Acknowledge God)*
10 your kingdom come, your will be done, *(Pray God's Will)*
on earth as it is in heaven.
11 Give us today our daily bread. *(Acknowledge God's Promises)*
12 And forgive us our debts,
as we also have forgiven our debtors. *(Ask for Forgiveness)*
13 And lead us not into temptation, *(Seek his Direction)*
but deliver us from the evil one.'" *(Seek his Protection)*

This example, given by Jesus of how to pray, is a model in which our prayers to the Father can be prayed. Jesus first acknowledged God for who He was as a sign of reverence. You may come to find that after spending time adoring God at the start of your prayer, the circumstances you were bringing to Him become lighter. What if you are battling sickness? You can start the prayer of adoration with, "God, thank You for being a healer, a comforter, my peace, a way maker, a doctor, etc." You have just placed God above your sickness! Next, Jesus prayed according to God's will; through this study, we have identified that we can recognize what God's will is by reading His Word. Jesus then went on to ask God for the promise that we reviewed in week three. The will of God that you have meditated on over the last few weeks and the promises that you have read in your daily reading are what can be used in your communication with God. Jesus also asked God for forgiveness acknowledging His understanding that sin is what hinders us from that intimate encounter. Not that Christ committed any sin, instead, He was aware of the existence of sin. For us, however, we have sinned so whatever sin is in your life is what can be used at this time in the prayer. An example of this can be, "God, forgive me for anything I did today that is contrary to your will for my life, and forgive me for anything that I have thought that is not aligned with who You say I am." Lastly, God's direction and protection was petitioned by Christ. Whatever it is that you are petitioning God for, it is important that you ask for it in line with His will. God's will for your life comes with direction and protection. Yes, your prayers come with an insurance policy!

Group Activity:

Break off into groups of 3-4. Take a moment of silence and meditation to reverently position yourself beyond the veil that was torn. Using what you read in the Bible as a foundation to acknowledging God's will, begin by first acknowledging God, then pray God's will, speak His promises, ask for forgiveness, and seek His direction and protection. Practice allowing yourself to be open to God's presence and willingness to hear from you.

Challenge:

Find a prayer partner this week to pray with. Also, carve time in every day to go beyond the veil and press for the encounter with God. Be vulnerable and specific about what is on your heart. Remember, in everything by prayer and petition, make your request known to God.

Moment of Honesty:

What area of your life do you need to lay down before God? If God could work out any area of your life, what would it be? Lay it down beyond the veil. What was that first thought? The beauty is that you do not have to share it with the group. This is when you accept God's proposal of having an intimate encounter between you and Him.

Memory Verse:
Psalm 18:6

Prayer:

God, thank You for caring enough about us to strategically plan for the veil to be torn. You are holy, God, and we are so undeserving to come before You, but You call us anyway. As we accept the challenge this week, make the 18th Psalm true in our lives. Whatever it is that we are harboring or in need of deliverance from, God, hear our cry! Convict us, God, to be mindful of our requests to You. Help us to match what is in our hearts and what we want with what we read in Your word. Allow us to increase our abilities to apply Your word, and will, to our prayers so that what we ask is pleasing to You. Forgive us, God, and grant us direction and protection! From Your temple, hear our voices. Amen.

Journal:

_____

_____

_____

_____

_____

_____

_____

_____

_____

_____

Last Week Flashback

How consistent were you last week in being intentional about praying? If you are willing, describe the experience you had when you prayed alone and with a partner? What are some of the challenges you face when it comes to praying?

Week Five

Hearing from God

Often times, after we have prayed about something that requires a response from God, we find ourselves in a place of uncertainty. In that unsure place, we can become impatient in waiting for a response, so much so, that we begin conversing with other sources and allowing their opinions to influence our judgment. The question that is often asked is, "How do I know I am hearing from God?" In John 10, we read that Jesus is the Good Shepherd and we are His sheep. The sheep hear and know His voice. How would you describe God's voice? Is it soft? Loud? Crystal clear? Does God speak in the same way every time He responds to you?

Elijah was a prophet of God introduced to us in 1 Kings 17. A task of a prophet was to hear from God and inform God's people of what was heard. Let's use the illustration of Elijah as our guide. The story of Elijah in 1 Kings 18 and 19 gives us a few examples of how God speaks. Within these two chapters, we find four tips on confirming God's voice:

1. God speaks through the testing of faith (1 Kings 18:20-39)
2. God speaks through provision (1 Kings 19:1-9)

3. God's response is accompanied by peace (1 Kings 19:10-13)

4. God's response aligns with His will (1 Kings 19:16;19-21)

Group Activity:

At this point in our journey to encounter God, we have learned how to read and apply the Bible. Using these skills, break off into four groups with each group taking one of the four tips. Read, comprehend, and apply how the context of the scriptures can help you determine God's voice from other voices. You can use the notes section to guide your thinking.

Group 1

God speaks through the testing of faith:

Elijah was able to dismiss the argument of people with the testing of what they told him to be true. Their approach leads to work and no response. Elijah then tested what he believed to be true through prayer, sacrifice, and seeing his prayer manifest into reality. Notice how Elijah prayed. Does his approach look familiar? (1 Kings 18:20-39)

Other examples:

Genesis 22: Abraham and Isaac

1 Kings 17: Elijah and the Widow

Group 2:

God speaks through provision:

Elijah was at the point of giving up. He cried out to God that he might die. God told him that he needed him to live by providing him with the resources he needed to carry on. Provision is not to be mistaken as always having what you think you need. God's provision does not work like that. God gives us provision in His own timing. It is through His provisions that we are able to confirm that God directed us to do what we heard. (1 Kings 19:1-9)

Other examples:

Genesis 22: Abraham and Isaac

1 Kings 17: Elijah and the Widow

Group 3:

God's response is accompanied by peace:

When God speaks, it will be clear to you as an individual. 1 Corinthians 14:33 says that God is not a God of confusion, but of peace. At this point in scripture, God had spoken through the wind, earthquakes, and fire, but Elijah had a peace and a knowing about the whisper which led him to show his external reverence to God. When you hear from God, there will be a peace in His response. Whether the response is comforting or scary, there will be a peace. Philippians 4:7 reminds us that the peace of God surpasses all understanding. (1 Kings 19:10-13)

Group 4:

God's response aligns with His will:

When God uses people as a source to respond to us, the response will align with the plans of God. God used Moses to bring His children out of Egypt and then asked Moses to pass the baton to Joshua to lead the children to the Promised Land. God, furthermore, used Elijah to oppose the worship of false gods. Elijah was then sent to pass the baton to Elisha to further complete God's work. When you hear God's voice, you will be able to confirm it with your prayers, provision, a spirit of peace, and the will God has for His sheep. (1 Kings 19:16;19-21) God's will always points back to His glory and redemption plan for humanity.

Group Discussion

Come back together and have a representative from each group share with the entire group how to hear from God.

Challenge:

Be intentional about carving out a time or times, with limited distraction, to listen to God. Allow your heart to release the uncertainty and confusion about your specific concern. Be still and know that He is God, as written in Psalm 46:10. Ask God to speak to you, and listen.

"The word listen contains the same letters as the word silent."

~Alfred Brendel

Moment of Honesty:

What are some of the things you have prayed for? Do they align with God's will? Do you have an example of a response you feel God has given you to a prayer? Have you tested it? Has God made provision for His instruction? Do you have peace about it? Does it align with God's will? If not, it is okay to revisit it and take it back to God in prayer. If all these things line up, reflect on how hearing from God can increase your faith in Him.

Memory Verse:
Jeremiah 33:3

Prayer:

God, thank You for being a God that speaks. Thank You for not only speaking to us but for also giving us the privilege and ability to hear from You. It states in Proverbs 2 that if we cry aloud for understanding and look for it as we would look for hidden treasure, we will find it. So God, as we position ourselves this week to hear from You, speak to us according to Your will for our lives. You promised us that if we ask for wisdom and understanding, You will give it to us. Forgive us for anything we have done thus far that is outside of Your will for our lives. Realign our thoughts, posture, and heart. Give us direction on the matters of our hearts so that we can live lives that glorify You. Protect us from the wolves and negative responses we hear and make our ears sensitive to Your voice God. Speak to us and give us the peace that surpasses all understanding as we stand still in Your presence. Amen.

Journal:

_____

_____

_____

_____

_____

_____

_____

_____

_____

_____

Last Week Flashback

How does hearing from God relate to reading and applying the Bible? Have you had an experience when you confidently heard from God? How would you describe the peace that proceeds hearing from God?

Week Six
Worshiping

So far, we have talked about how in reading the Bible, we are able to expand our knowledge base of who God is. We then went on to apply the knowledge of God to our daily lives. Through our application, we find purpose and reason to pray and hear from God. Although each of these topics has unique definitions, they all have a common denominator - revering or showing adoration to God.

So what exactly is worship? Worship, by definition, is the feeling or expression of reverence and adoration for a deity. Recognizing that God is the deity in which we are to feel and show reverence and adoration to is the place where true worship flows from. With this breakdown of worship, we are no longer limited to needing music, a church building, or a ministry to serve in to worship God. While all of these things are important and create a greater sense of intimacy in worship, they by definition do not define worship. Worship is a lifestyle in which everything you say, think, or do can express your reverence and adoration to God. In fact, the place your heart is in as we read this study *is* worship! A beautiful thing about worship is that we are invited into it by God. In John 4:10, we see Jesus inviting a woman into a posture of worship. This woman was trapped in a mental prison that her culture and life choices placed her in. She lacked the understanding of who to reverence and had a hard time opening her mind beyond what she had already been exposed to. Jesus reveals to her, Himself, and speaks to areas in her life that are unclean. He challenged her to serve Him (vs. 7), believe in Him (vs. 10), thirst for Him (vs. 14), and be honest with Him (vs. 18). Jesus concludes with the woman by informing her that He wants her to worship Him in spirit and in truth (John 4:23). You can worship God in spirit and in truth through honesty, a declaration of who God is, and the acceptance of His invitation. Whether you are in your home, at work, or in the middle of a worship set on Sunday morning, worship can take place. How so? By centering your heart to accept Jesus' invitation, confessing, and then declaring who God is, which will lift Him higher than you and your circumstance. A passage of scripture that illustrates these steps can be found in John 4:7-23.

Group Activity

Instructions: *Prior to the start of the group, prepare 3 slips of paper with the word READ, 3 with the word APPLY, and 3 with the word PRAY. Attach slips onto various chairs in the group. During the activity, those with a slip will follow its instructions to break down the passage. Group members can trade slips if both parties agree. Those with Apply or Pray can call on Life Line support if necessary.* **Group activity passage:** John 4:7-23 *Begin by having one person with a Pray slip pray for the reading of God's Word. Have those with the Read slip read aloud this passage. Then have one person pray that the Spirit of God aid the group in understanding and applying this passage. The Apply slip individuals will vocalize their understanding and application. Close with the third person praying.*

Group Discussion

Instructions: *The group collectively will alternate sharing what they received (HEAR) from God in this lesson.*

1. In what verses of this passage do we see the invitation to worship?
2. In verse 11, what was hindering the woman from understanding who she was supposed to worship?
3. How do verses 16-19 show us the significance of honesty and vulnerability in worship?
4. How would not being honest prevent us from having true worship?
5. What does a moment in true worship feel like?
6. What are some ways that you can express your worship to God?

Challenge:

Take time out to worship God in spirit and in truth. The woman at the well had to let go of her past and admit to Jesus her truth. In identifying that, He was able to see her for who she was. She then could reverence Him for who He was in her life. Be honest with God and when He speaks, accept His invitation!

Moment of Honesty:

What circumstance in your life can you use to relate to the woman at the well? For her, it was her promiscuity. What is it that will hinder your worship experience from being one of spirit and truth?

Memory Verse:
John 4:23

Prayer:

God, we thank You for being the well that never runs dry. We acknowledge that You are worthy of receiving worship that is true. Forgive us for allowing our past and sin to hinder our reverence and adoration towards You. Clean our hearts with Your purification system. Speak to us in areas that others are afraid to, or that we are even afraid to admit to ourselves. You honor worshippers who worship You in spirit and in truth. God allow Your Spirit to dwell in our hearts, minds, and actions so that our worship is pleasing to You and ultimately makes You smile. Help us, this week, to reflect on how we worship and how we can better worship You. Create moments for us that we can be intentional in revering You. Help us to feel and express who You are. Protect us from the temptation of worshiping idols and lead us back to You as the good shepherd does his sheep. We accept Your invitation, God, and trust that in this space we will get to know You more. Amen.

Journal:

Last Week Flashback

How has the definition of worship impacted your life? What does it mean to worship God in spirit and in truth? Name one way you worshiped God in the past week.

Week Seven
Walking with God

How can two walk together unless they agree? Sack racing is a game that you can find many people of different ages playing on a warm spring or summer day. The object of the game is to get to a destination with the person beside you. The challenge lies in the coordination and communication between the two individuals. If both individuals make an agreement on when to jump and where to jump, the chances are they will swiftly get to the destination. On the contrary, if the two do not agree on these specifics, they will fall and ultimately travel nowhere fast! The same holds true when walking with God.

Over the course of the last five weeks, we have grown to know God through the reading of His Word, applying His Word, communicating with Him, and living a life of worship. At some point, you had to decide whether or not you agree with Him. It is in the agreement that we can begin walking with God in the direction He is calling us to.

"Amen" is used in our faith as a verbal indication of agreement. Have you said Amen to God's Word?! When God says, "Jump, on the count of 3," will you jump or will you prolong the journey He is taking you on? Walking with God is not necessarily a fearless journey, but it is, in fact, worth every step.

So, is walking with God as simple as agreeing with Him? Not exactly. It requires you making the conscious decision to have the effort and will to move with Him. Walking with God takes courage to accept what He says and action to take steps in places possibly unknown to you. We can find comfort in knowing that God promised to walk with us. Leviticus 26:12 reads, "I will also walk among you and be your God, and you shall be my people."

There are three scenarios that can teach us about our decisions on walking with God. The choices made in these scenarios, much like sack racing, determines the progress we will or will not make in our relationship with God. Let's look at the lives of Adam & Eve, Jonah, and Daniel to paint an illustration of decisions, results, and how we can choose to walk with God.

Scenarios

1. Adam & Eve
    a. Walk and Yielding to Temptation
    b. Genesis 2:15-17; 3:6-10; 3:21-23

2. Jonah
    a. Running Away from Walking
    b. Jonah 1:1-12; 1:15-17; 3:1-3

3. Daniel
    a. Walking with Boldness
    b. Daniel 1:3-17

Group Activity

This group activity will incorporate *Reading, Praying, Applying, and Worship*. Separate into three groups. With each group member participating, answer the following questions for your assigned scenario.

1. What decision had to be made here?

2. What was the choice that was made?

3. What were the results of the choice that was made?

4. What is an example of this choice in the context of our lives now?

5. (Worship) What characteristics of God is being revealed in this scenario?

Group Discussion

Have a group leader give the answers to each scenario. We see in the scenarios that walking with God is a choice.

1. What type of decisions are we faced with today?
2. How do the choices we make effect our relationship with God?
3. What have been some of the results of the choices we made?
4. What are some scriptures that align with the choices you have made?

Challenge:

Think about the upcoming week or month. What decisions do you have to make? Write a list of the decisions and in a column next to them, write down a scripture that agrees with the choice.

Moment of Honesty:

Think about some of the choices you have made. Who do you relate to the most, Adam & Eve, Jonah, or Daniel? What boundaries can you put in place so that temptation won't prevent you from moving forward with God? What scriptures can you use and meditate on to redirect yourself when you feel like running?

Memory Verse:

Psalm 119:1

Prayer:

God, thank You for choosing to walk with us daily. Thank You for using our lives for the purpose of Your kingdom. God, we acknowledge that You give instruction to us and that Your expectations of us are threaded through the scriptures. Speak clearly to us and help us make choices that are in agreement with Your Word. Help us to flee from temptation for we know that it only leads to shame, fear, and distance from You. God, also help us to not fear or doubt Your plan for us. Help us not to flee from Your calling like Jonah did, causing those around us to be affected. God, teach us to walk like Daniel, bold and secure in his relationship to the one true God. Forgive us of anything we have done up to now that has distanced us from You. Help us to grab hold of Your truth and walk side by side with You until Your work in us is made complete. Amen.

Journal:

_____

_____

_____

_____

_____

_____

_____

_____

_____

_____

Last Week Flashback

Out of the six areas discussed, up to now, how do they all relate to having an encounter with God? What new insight has been gained in these areas? What area(s) do you still need more clarification in?

Week Eight
Trusting God

Consider for a moment, you are entering into a new relationship whether it is a working, romantic, or peer relationship. The art of getting to know someone leads to a conclusion of whether or not you can or will trust them. Trusting in the context of human relationships does not mean that you believe this person will never fail you, but that you believe this person is honest and sincere. You can trust that your job will pay you every two weeks, and based on that trust, you perform on a job for an average of 80 hours in that two-week span. Additionally, you can trust that if a new romantic interest said they would meet you at a restaurant, they would show up and with that trust, you would drive to the destination. What if the organization you work for gets shut down or the date stands you up? Putting our trust in systems or people is risky, but we do it every day. In fact, you put your trust in the chair you are sitting in right now. Unconsciously, you believed the chair would hold you up as you sat down.

Evaluating trust, in this way, suggests that trust translates into our behaviors. How we speak about something or conduct ourselves in everyday circumstances is a reflection of what or who we put our trust in. Proverbs 3:5 reads, "Trust in the Lord with all of your heart and lean not to your own understanding." Let's take a moment to glance back at the woman at the well from week six. When she leaned to her own understanding, it hindered her from relying on Jesus. When she opened her heart to His truth, she was able to shake off what she had believed from her past experiences and walk into a secure relationship with Jesus. In order for our trust in God to be translated into our speaking and conduct, we have to let go of what the world tells us is true and speak the Word of God. After speaking the Word of God, we must then match our behaviors to what we spoke, which is our application. Taking these steps will build confidence and ultimately shift your lifestyle. Your trust in God, lastly, leads to you impacting those around you. The peace that you will carry and the confidence you will wear, seamed together with the faithfulness of God, will be an indirect witness of God to all those who know you.

Over a year ago, I was in a season of asking God to confirm if He wanted me to stay in the location I was in or if it was in His will that I seek employment somewhere else. On one of my days off, I was driving what I thought was the speed limit from a dental appointment to an eye appointment and got pulled over for speeding. To you, that may or may not be a big deal, but for me, it was my third ticket and suddenly my heart dropped. I knew that this third ticket would put me in violation of my company policy. Long story short, the judge did not drop the charges and I was forced to resign from my job. A large percentage of the people I shared this story with were fearful, sad, upset, wanting to defend me, and coming up with solutions on what I should do next. As for me, it was a trying time, yes, but it was also an opportunity to trust God and perplex people! I stood firm in my faith and remembered everything I said "Amen" to in church and willed myself not to panic. Six months later, I was living in a different state with a new job. This was a great example of God speaking through peace and provision. I trusted God's word and will, and it did not go back to Him void.

How to trust God

1. Know the truth (Reading)
2. Speak the truth (Worshipping and Praying)
3. Apply truth through our actions (Applying and Walking)

Group Activity

As we have journeyed through this series, we gained the understanding that scripture is a guide to our relationship with God that provides us with a variety of examples. Last week, we looked into the life of Daniel and found that his walk with God reflected boldness and commitment. This week, we will look into how Daniel's friends displayed their trust in God. You will be challenged in your personal time to compare an experience Daniel has later in scripture, to the experience we will unfold as a group. Using the weekly lessons on *Reading, Applying, Praying, Worshipping, and Walking with God*, unpack the following story.

Passage of Scripture: Daniel 3: 16-30

Applying - Interpret the reading

1. What truth is used as the foundation of their trust in God?
2. What method did they use to speak this truth?
3. They had on several garments that, by the world's intellect, would decrease their chances of survival. Why did they survive, but those who put them in the furnace died?

Worshipping - Showing reverence and adoration to God

1. What attributes of God are found in this story to show reverence or adoration?

Walking - Having courage to accept the journey God has you on

1. How was courage displayed in this story?
2. What decisions had to be made in this story?
3. Why is there a fourth person in the furnace?
4. What did these men give up to walk with God?
5. What were the results of the choice that was made?

Group Discussion

1. What are some examples of modern day fiery furnaces?
2. If you have ever experienced a modern day fiery furnace, what did you do to get into one?
3. What are some examples of how we can trust God, today, in furnace like circumstances?
4. How can our trust in God, during fiery times, be used as a witness to others?

Challenge:

Read Daniel, chapter 6. Using the guide from the group activity, respond to this chapter by reading, praying, applying, worshipping, and walking. Use your responses, this week, as a foundation for increasing your trust in God as it relates to your *moment of honesty* answer.

Moment of Honesty:

What are you faced with, today, that you need to trust God in? Do you know God's truth as it relates to what you have identified? How can you challenge yourself to begin speaking the truth and acting in ways that reflect the truth(s) you found?

Memory Verse:

Proverbs 3:5

Prayer:

God, thank You for being a God that we can trust. You have shown Yourself to be faithful in the scriptures and even in our lives. You are there walking with us through the valley, as well as the mountain top. Help us to find Your truth as it relates to our circumstances. In Your word, it tells us to take captive every thought and make it obedient to You. So God, as thoughts of what we cannot accomplish enters our minds, speak truth to us so that we can replace wrong with right. We want to trust in You with all of our hearts and lean not to our understanding. Forgive us for speaking and conducting ourselves as the world and help us down the straight path You have for us as we trust you. We ask and believe all of this in your Son Jesus' name. Amen.

Journal:

_____

_____

_____

_____

_____

_____

_____

_____

_____

_____

_____

Week Nine
Flashback

Whether you are reading the Bible or conversing with a friend over coffee, the probability that relationships will be discussed is extremely high. The relationship topic itself is universal, and I would argue, is the reason why it is used countless times in scripture. A relationship is something we can all comprehend on one level or another, and it can be used to apply meaning and understanding to the context of a variety of issues. To push the thought even further, one could have a negative relationship or a positive relationship with someone and that encounter between the two individuals would have a lasting influence. Considering all the relationships discussed in history and in the context of scriptures, there is one relationship encounter that we can have that will not let us down. In fact, the encounter we have with God will be or should be the foundation in which all other relationships are cultivated.

Over the last several weeks, we have interacted with God through reading His Word, applying it, talking with Him, hearing back from Him, acknowledging who He is, walking with Him, and trusting Him. The outcome of these interactions with God has, in some way or another, impacted your life. Our faith in God should not be lived out as a religion, but as a developing relationship. Religion is how someone practices what they believe and can become mundane and stressful to carry out consistently. A relationship, however, has a foundation of beliefs as well, but is something that is always growing and crystalizing. There is one way to act out a specific religion, but there is not one way to carry out a relationship. When we learn to work out a relationship with God by increasing our knowledge, communicating, and acting in ways that are consistent with the foundational beliefs, we can then use this same framework in building and managing relationships with others. The journey of encountering God does not stop at the end of this series, but continues throughout eternity. Each study, used in these last several weeks, are like the ingredients of a cake. Each has its own unique purpose in building the relationship; alone, they do not create the completed results. Blending these ingredients together and giving them time to form will result in an effective growing relationship and encounter with God.

This journey has taught us that we, as God's children, can have life and have it to the fullest. We have the privilege to be in this type of relationship with Him because He laid down His life for us - as a good shepherd does. In order to believe this, though, we learned that we must first read it for ourselves. The King James Version of 2 Timothy 2:15 reads, "Study to show thyself approved unto God, a workman that needeth not to be ashamed, rightly dividing the Word of truth." After reading the Word, we are then to be careful to do everything written in it. Joshua 1:8 reminds us of this, "Do not let this Book of the Law depart from your mouth; meditate on it day and night, so that you may be careful to do everything that is written in it. Then you will be prosperous and successful." Consider the studies we have completed: Joshua, Elijah, the woman at the well, Daniel and all three of his friends engaged in praying, hearing from God, worshipping, walking with God, and trusting God in their encounter with Him. Who will you read about next? How will you apply these ingredients to the next phase of your life?

Group Discussion

1. What was the most impactful topic/week for you in this study?
2. Do you feel as though putting these areas to practice have ushered you into an encounter with God?
3. How does experiencing God for yourself impact your comfort and ability to usher someone else into an experience with God?

Moment of Honesty:

In the first week, you were asked to reflect on where you were in each area and identify ways in which you could improve. Complete this exercise again. Has anything changed? What are you still working towards? Who is going to be your accountability partner in your journey with God?

Prayer:

God, thank You for inviting us to experience You. You created the heavens and the earth and deemed it beneficial to create man and You did so in Your image and likeness. It was the sin of humanity that separated us from Your presence. Because You are the Good Shepherd, You laid down Your life so that we may experience You again. Help us to keep the relationship we have with You at the center of our lives. Convict us when we go astray and remind us that Your Word is available, communicating with You is vital, worshipping You is commanded, and trusting You will lead us down straight paths. Forgive us for not doing things Your way and compromising with the ways and understanding of the world. We want to walk with You and hear from You. Do not turn a death ear to us, oh God. We declare that Your Word is true and that we will be obedient to our call to follow You and show others how to follow You as well. This we ask and pray in Jesus' name. Amen.

Journal:

_____

_____

_____

_____

_____

_____

_____

_____

_____

_____

_____

CPSIA information can be obtained
at www.ICGtesting.com
Printed in the USA
FFOW02n1107130317
33344FF